Inspired by

Great Grace Network Bible Club

For ages 7-15

Presented to

Presented by

Date

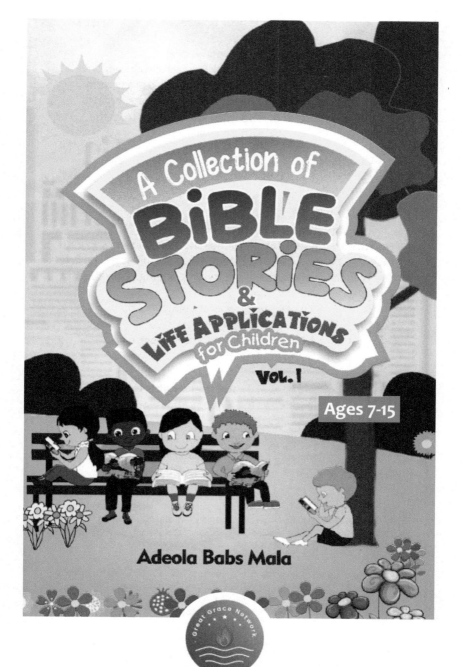

A Collection of

BiBLE STORIES

&

LIFE APPLICATIONS

for Children

VOL. 1

Ages 7-15

Adeola Babs Mala

ISBN: 9798828839407

Inspired by Great Grace Network Bible Club
Great Grace Network is a non-denominational ministry outreach
based in Calgary, Alberta and is dedicated to igniting, rekindling,
sustaining and spreading revival fire among believers.

www.greatgracenetwork.com
+1 (403) 926-7191
Email: bibleclub@greatgracenetwork.com

**Adeola Babs Mala asserts her rights to be
identified as the author of this work.**

Illustrator – Emmanuel O. Taiwo
Cover art idea – Daniel and David Babs Mala
Layout design and consulting partner – **Purplebloom**

Dedication

This book is dedicated to the children, past, present, and future, of Great Grace Bible Club, Calgary, Canada, whom I had the grace of God to teach some of the lessons contained in this book and who inspired me to pass it on to a wider audience of the children of the world, both born and unborn.

I love you all and I believe you are going places for Christ.

Contents

Acknowledgments

To God, the Father of all grace, I thank you for the opportunity to be a vessel of honour in your hands.

I sincerely appreciate my dear husband, Pastor (Dr) Tolu Mala, for his love, support, and encouragement. My glorious sons, David Jesunifemi and Daniel Jesuferanmi, for being my inspiration every step along the way.

I want to thank my parents, Professor (Pastor) and Elder (Mrs) John Adeniyi and Bolupe Mojirayo Fagbenro, who, while we were very young, said YES to every opportunity that presented itself to learn about Christ. Thank you, Dad, for your invaluable editorial work and other constructive contributions to this book.

I want to especially appreciate my eldest sister, Oluwafemi, fondly called sister, who introduced Christ to my older sister and me at a very young age. That was the beginning of my faith journey. She also helped to edit the raw manuscript of this book. Thank you, big sister!

I use this opportunity to express gratitude to my primary (Grade) 2 teachers, Mrs Bola Ogundipe (Adebiyi) and Mrs Bola Adepoju, who took care of my younger brother Oluniyi and me when we attended our first Bible camp at the Oritamefa Baptist Church Easter camp in Awe, Oyo State. This meeting ignited my love for Jesus Christ!

I am eternally grateful to Mrs Iyabo Anisulowo, who introduced my family to Faith Clinic Nigeria Inc and Word Communication Ministries (WOCOM). My love for God grew stronger and I made destiny relationships through these ministries. Thank you to Aunty Olo Adedeji, who taught me at the Roots Conference organised by WOCOM and wrote this book's foreword.

Architect (Mrs) Bolaji Adeniyi gave me a firsthand experience of neighbourhood Bible Club at Idi-Ishin/Jericho axis in Ibadan, Nigeria. She brought together children from the area to her house to learn at the feet of Jesus. The lessons learned there shaped the lives of many of us and I am a testament to this. I acknowledge her for a job well done. Thank you for giving to the Lord!

A big shout out to all my folks at The Happiest Children on Earth Fellowship, Jericho, Ibadan, which was started as an offshoot of the other neighbourhood Bible club when the Adeniyis moved to another location. One love keep us together!

I acknowledge the mentorship of Aunty Ren over the years. You are appreciated.

Many thanks to Emmanuel O. Taiwo for working on the Illustrations.

I thank my siblings and their spouses, my in-laws and extended family, my local church family, Great Grace Network, and my colleagues at work for all their contributions and support.

Foreword

This handbook is a well-illustrated and colourful compilation of Bible stories that bring the Bible closer to the child and endears it to him or her. The child is made to relate to the happenings in graphic scenes. Besides the beautiful and vivid illustrations, the handbook covers a comprehensive list of topics from understanding sin, keeping away from it, the need for salvation, trusting and depending on God, separation from the devil, being beacons of light and total obedience to God. Other areas covered include giving thanks, forgiveness, preference for godly counsel, the quest for excellence, good behaviour, loving God and living daily to please Him. All these topics seek to build the total child, leaving no stone unturned in his or her Christian pilgrimage.

This handbook is made further interesting by the Bible characters used to teach moral lessons. For example, Nicodemus highlights the need to be born again; Joseph is used to show why we must shun sin and Shadrach, Meshach, and Abednego show the need to trust God. David and the story of the Amalekites demonstrate the importance of being led by God. Barnabas and Paul show the relevance of the Holy Spirit in evangelism. Solomon is used to illustrate the danger embedded in an unequal yoke. Abraham is used to teach the child the advantage that lies in making obedience to God a priority, while Rehoboam demonstrates the disaster that lies in shunning godly counsel.

Noah teaches the need for prompt obedience to God's commands. Saul dramatizes the unwholesomeness of incomplete obedience to God's laws. Joshua is used to teach the gains of consistent obedience to God. Peter's sermon on the day of Pentecost teaches the gains of being strong, and bold in ministry. Daniel's interpretation of the king's dream highlights relying on God for wisdom and insight. Dorcas is used to teach the dividends of generosity while Joshua and Caleb illustrate the need for optimism in our attitude to crisis. Gideon is used to reflect that "no matter your physical weakness or position of inadequacy," God can strengthen you.

All told, this handbook is a goldmine in the lessons it brings to the fore for any child-Christian or otherwise. In its content, it is maximally rich. You can see the author's passionate desire for righteous living in children.

In all of my five decades of Christian children evangelism, this handbook stands out clearly as one of the best materials that make teaching children a delight. It is a job very well done. It is picturesque and easy to handle, yet it is detailed, well thought out and structured. It is a brilliant literal piece and a blessing not only to this generation but to many more to come.

It is a must-read for children, parents, teachers, and all others. This is a work assiduously accomplished and hereby highly recommended. The gains from reading it are innumerable.

Happy reading!

Olohigbe Adedeji (Ph.D)
Coordinator, Aunty Olo Children's Ministry

Introduction

When the Great Grace Network Bible Club started a couple of years ago, the pioneer children were taught practical Bible lessons with songs. In apparent response to the very interesting and beneficial nature of the lessons, the children wanted a story dimension to be added to their lessons. According to them, this would further drive home the points and make them more applicable. I responded positively to the yearning of the children, and the result was amazing.

Later on, the Lord began to lay in my heart the need to document these lessons in the form of a book. My obedience to the leading of the Holy Spirit gave birth to this book which is the first in the series of *A Collection of Bible Stories and Life Applications for Children*.

I therefore present this first edition to the millennials, their parents, guardians, and mentors with great joy.

I pray that it fulfills its purpose, which is to simplify biblical truths for the spiritual growth, edification, and reading enjoyment of Christian children as well as adults who want to be converted as children to train them in the way of the Lord.

Matthew 18:3 NLT, then he said, "I tell you the truth, unless you turn from your sins and become like little children, you will never get into the Kingdom of Heaven."

Adeola Babs Mala
Calgary, AB
April 2022

Be Born Again!

Bible Story: John 3:1-7 (Nicodemus asked about the new birth)

Memory Verse: Verily, verily I say unto you, except a man be born again, he cannot see the kingdom of God. (John 3:3 NKJV)

The Story

1. Nicodemus was a Jewish religious leader. He was a Pharisee.

2. Pharisees believed in following lawful traditions.

3. Nicodemus went to Jesus at night and called Jesus Rabbi, which means teacher.

4. He said that he knew that the miraculous signs following Jesus were evidence that God was with Him.

5. Nicodemus asked Him how a man could be born again after being born by his mother.

6. Jesus told him that, to seek the Kingdom of God, He must be born by water (God's word) and by the Holy Spirit.

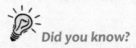

Did you know?

Pharisees were the only legal experts during the time of Jesus that believed in the resurrection from the dead.

Meditation

1. The new birth is basic to the Christian faith.

2. It means confessing our sins, genuinely repenting of them, and accepting Jesus Christ as our Lord and saviour.

3. If you are yet to give your life to Jesus, accepting Him as your personal Lord and Saviour is important to becoming a Christian.

4. Going to church with parents, siblings, and friends without new birth will not earn you salvation.

5. You have to make a personal commitment to accept Jesus into your heart.

6. Confessing with your mouth that He is the Lord and believing that God raised Him from the dead on the third day is the foundation of the Christian life.

7. We are not saved by trying so hard to be good.

8. Being good is not the same as being saved, even though being saved will make you behave well.

9. Being saved by accepting Jesus makes being good a normal lifestyle for you.

10. If you are not yet born again and you want to be born again, say these prayers after me:

Dear Jesus, I know you love me, and that is why you left heaven to come and die for me on the cross of Calvary so I can be saved. I accept you as my personal Lord and Saviour today. Forgive me all my sins. Write my name in the Book of Life. Come into my heart to stay in Jesus' name. Amen

11 If you just said that prayer, you are saved and now born again. Keep reading God's word (the Bible) and pray every day. Attend a church where the word of God is being preached rightly. Fellowship with other Christians regularly.

12 Being of good behaviour will be a normal daily experience for you since Jesus is already in you.

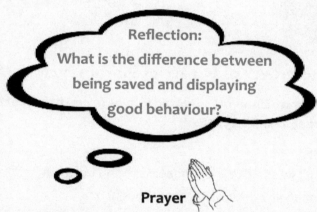

Reflection:
What is the difference between being saved and displaying good behaviour?

Prayer

Dear Lord, I rededicate my life to you. Help me to continue to love you and do only those things that make you happy daily in Jesus' name. Amen

Run Away from Sin!

Bible Story: Genesis 39:1-21 (Joseph runs away from sin)

Memory Verse: Thy word have I hid in mine heart that I might not sin against thee. (Psalm 119:11 KJV)

The Story

1. Joseph was sold to the Ishmaelites by his brothers.

2. Potiphar, an officer of Pharaoh, bought him.

3. The Lord was with Joseph, and everything he did prospered. So, his boss kept him in charge of his whole household.

4. Potiphar's wife liked Joseph and wanted to have an unholy affair with him, but Joseph said NO!

5. She pestered Joseph several times to force him to commit a huge sin, but Joseph ran away from her.

6. Potiphar's wife lied against Joseph to her husband and told him that Joseph wanted to force her to have an affair with him.

7. Potiphar sent Joseph to prison because he thought that what his wife told him was true.

8. The Lord was still with Joseph even in prison because he was innocent.

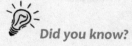

Did you know?

Joseph was the most beloved son of Jacob.
His father made him a coat of many colours.

Meditation

1. Every day of our lives, we are faced with various situations and temptations.

2. We should never give in, just like Joseph did not give in.

3. Instead, we should run away from those circumstances as far away as possible.

4. God's word in our hearts gives us the strength to say NO to sin.

5. Sin is an offence against God.

6. Sin puts a gap between God and us.

7. Sin makes God sad.

8. When we find ourselves in an unpleasant situation, we should not remain there.

9. We should use every strength we have to fight and run away from sin.

10. A little compromise can land us in great trouble.

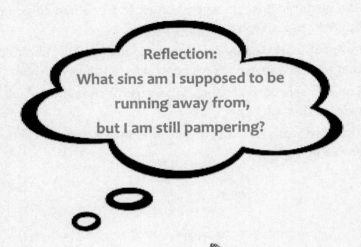

Reflection:
What sins am I supposed to be
running away from,
but I am still pampering?

Prayer

Gracious and merciful Father, there are many
invitations to sin that stare me in the face every
minute of the day. Help me to say NO and run away
from every temptation in Jesus' name. Amen

Study 3

Who is my Neighbour?

Bible Story: Luke 10:30-37 (The Good Samaritan's story)

Memory Verse: He who does not love does not know God, for God is love. (1 John 4:8 NKJV)

The Story

1. A Jewish man was traveling down to Jericho.

2. He was attacked by thieves who took all he had, beat him, and left him half dead.

3. A priest was passing by, saw him and then he crossed to the other side of the road and went away.

4. A Levite (temple assistant) was also passing by and moved closer, looked at him but also went on his way.

5. A Samaritan came, saw the man, and had compassion for Him.

6. He administered first aid with oil and wine and put the wound in a bandage.

7. He carried the man to a place where he could be taken care of.

8. He gave the people that were taking care of the man money and promised to pay more if needed on his return.

9. The Samaritan was the neighbour of the wounded man.

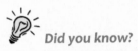 *Did you know?*

Samaritans are said to be Israelites from the Northern part of the land.

Meditation

1. Every day in our lives, we meet people in conditions where they cannot help themselves.

2. They may be people that do not share the same belief or religion with us. They may also be of a different race, gender etc.

3. We are expected to show them love and compassion just as Jesus taught us.

4. Being a Christian is first by our actions and not by mere words or the titles or offices we hold.

5. The priest and assistant pastor did not help the man who was robbed and wounded.

6. They only looked at him and passed by, pretending to be in a rush or they did not want their garments to be soiled.

7. The Samaritan who was considered not to be as religious as the

original Jews was full of kindness by coming to the rescue of the wounded man.

8. The other side of the story is that God, in His mightiness, could use any of His creatures to send us the timely help we need.

9. The help may be from people we think are not like us or do not share the same belief or religion as we have.

10. God is the creator of everyone, and He may decide to use any of His creations to help us.

11. We have to be open to God and hear Him and know where He wants us to go so that we will not fall victim to any mishap.

12. We must also obey Him by doing what His word says we must do to be a blessing to other people.

Reflection:
Who is my neighbour?

Prayer

Sovereign Lord, use me to help other people who might be struggling or in difficult situations around me. Father, I also ask that you send timely help to me whenever I need it through the people you might be sending my way and help me know whether you want me to accept such help in Jesus' name. Amen

Bible Story: Daniel 3:10-30 (The Hebrew boys were saved from the blazing furnace)

Memory Verse: Behold, I give you the authority to trample on serpents and scorpions and over all the power of the enemy, and nothing shall by any means hurt you. (Luke 10:19 NKJV)

The Story

1. King Nebuchadnezzar had issued a decree that all the people in the land should bow down and worship his gold statue at the sound of the musical instruments.

2. He also said those who refuse to obey must be thrown into a blazing furnace.

3. Some astrologers reported Shadrach, Meshach, and Abednego (the 3 Hebrew boys) to the king because they refused to worship the golden statue.

4. Although they were Hebrew and strangers in the land, they were provincial heads in Babylon.

5. The king ordered that they should be brought to him so that he might confirm their disobedience.

6. He gave them one more chance to bow down to his golden image, but they still said NO to the king.

7. They boldly declared that the Almighty God whom they were serving would deliver them from the blazing furnace.

8. They also declared that even if their God did not save them, they would still not bow to the statue or serve the king's gods.

9. The king was furious and commanded the furnace to be heated seven times hotter.

10. He commanded that they be bound and thrown into the furnace.

11. The furnace was so hot that the soldiers who threw the men into it got killed by the flames from the fire.

12. Later, the king went by the furnace and immediately noticed that four men were walking freely in the fire without being hurt.

13. He said the fourth man in the furnace looked like the son of the living God.

14. Immediately, the king commanded that the three Hebrew boys be freed and commanded that anyone who spoke against their God be destroyed.

15. They were also promoted to higher positions in the kingdom of Babylon.

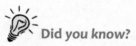 **Did you know?**

The actual Hebrew names of Shadrach,
Meshach and Abednego were Hananiah, Mishael and Azariah.

Meditation

1. The three Hebrew boys knew their God and chose to obey Him regardless of the type of punishment that might result from their decision.

2. As God's children, we should always choose to obey and trust God in the face of temptations and trials of faith that we face daily.

3. We are faced with choices either to go the wrong way (speak lies, deny our faith, join with people who are going the wrong way, etc.) or go the right way which is the way of the Lord.

4. We should always choose to obey God only, even if it is at the point of death.

5. God has promised to save us through every affliction, but even if He chooses not to do that at that point, He will save us on the last day so we can reign with him forever.

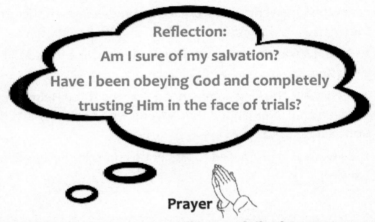

Reflection:

Am I sure of my salvation?

Have I been obeying God and completely trusting Him in the face of trials?

Prayer

Faithful God, I face many challenges daily that tempt me to deny my faith and disobey you. Dear Father, help me to always stand for you and you alone and refuse to bow down to the pressure of life in Jesus' name. Amen

Study 5

Recognise God in all your Ways

Bible Story: 1 Sam 30:1-30 (David follows God's direction to pursue)

Memory Verse: In all your ways, acknowledge him, and he shall direct your path. (Proverbs 3:6 NKJV)

The Story

1. David and his men arrived home at Ziklag and found that the Amalekites had raided their city.

2. They carried off everyone in the city.

3. David and his men wept until they were tired.

4. All the men were sad and wanted to kill David because they had nothing left.

5. David found strength in the Lord and asked Abiathar, the priest, to bring the Ephod, and David asked God questions.

6. God told him to go after the band of raiders; he would get everything that was taken.

7. They started the pursuit with 600 men, but 200 men were tired. He continued with the 400 men.

8. They saw a tired slave on the way who belonged to the Amalekites. They gave him some food and he told David that they were the ones that robbed Ziklag.

9. David asked him questions and promised that he would not leak the secret.

10. This man led David and his men to the Amalekites, and they got everything back that was taken plus some extras.

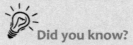

Did you know?

David had 30 mighty men and others

with whom he fought battles with.

Meditation

1. Sometimes, we can get to the point of fear, discouragement, and tiredness in life.

2. At this point, we should brace up, pray, and ask God for direction.

3. We should not call a pity party because this will only make the devil rejoice over us.

4. We should be like David, who encouraged himself in the Lord.

5. David asked what to do from God, and God told him to go and he would get everything back.

6. When we are in the middle of confusion, and it seems we do not know what to do or what choices we are to make, our trust should be in God and Him alone.

7. He has promised to direct our path and give us the victory we need when we trust in Him.

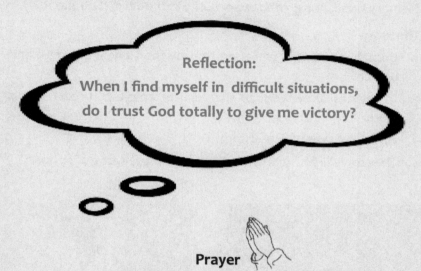

Reflection:
When I find myself in difficult situations,
do I trust God totally to give me victory?

Prayer

My Dear Saviour, when I am faced with difficult situations, I have many options to choose from, but I always want to get it right. I do not want to miss your direction for my life. Please direct my path as I trust in you in Jesus' name. Amen

Study 6

Give No Room to the Devil

Bible Story: Acts 13:4-12 (Apostle Paul rebuked Elymas)

Memory Verse: And give no opportunity to the devil. (Eph 4:27 RSV)

The Story

1. Barnabas and Paul were sent out by the Holy Spirit to go and preach.

2. In Salamis, they went to the Jewish temple to preach God's word.

3. John Mark was their assistant.

4. They travelled from town to town until they reached Paphos.

28

5. The governor invited Barnabas and Paul to visit him so that he could hear God's word.

6. There, they met a Jewish wizard, a false prophet named BarJesus, aka Elymas.

7. Elymas urged the governor not to listen to what Barnabas and Paul were saying.

8. He was trying to keep him from hearing the gospel of Jesus Christ and believing.

9. Paul, full of the Holy Spirit, rebuked the wizard, calling him all sorts of negative names and accused him of preventing people from hearing the word of God.

10. Paul commanded that he be blind immediately, needing someone to lead him by the hand.

11. When the governor heard the word of God and the miracle that happened, he gave his life to the Lord.

 *Did you know?*

Paul and Barnabas were together on
their missionary journey before each went
their separate ways.

Meditation

1. As young believers, it is essential that every step we take or any move we make must be led by the Holy Spirit.

2. We should also not spare the evil work of darkness when we see one.

3. In the narrative above, Elymas the wizard, stood in the governor's way by urging him not to listen to God's word.

4. He was opposing a man who was interested in knowing God.

5. Paul did not tolerate him but rebuked him sharply.

6. Whenever we see the devil's representative about to do an evil thing, we should give him no opportunity to perform.

7. We should speak out against evil with wisdom and not be silent.

8. God has given us boldness with the help of the Holy Spirit to stand against evil.

9. We should not allow the devil to use us for his devilish work.

10. He disguises himself sometimes as a good person, so we must pray to distinguish between good and evil.

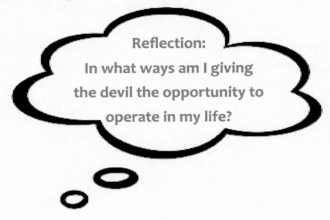

Reflection:

In what ways am I giving the devil the opportunity to operate in my life?

Prayer

Dear Lord, you know I love you and dislike the devil. Help me never to give the devil the opportunity to operate in my life in Jesus' name. Amen

Bible Story:1 Kings 11:1-6 (Solomon married many wives and turned his back on God)

Memory Verse: Do not be unequally yoked together with unbelievers. For what fellowship has righteousness with lawlessness? And what communion has light with darkness? (2 Corinthians 6:14 NKJV)

The Story

1. King Solomon loved many strange women.
2. He married from Egypt, Moab, Ammon, Edom, Sidon, and the Hittites.

3. The Lord had clearly instructed the Israelites not to marry such women because they would turn their hearts away from the true God to their gods.
4. Solomon disobeyed and insisted on doing the opposite.
5. He had 700 wives and 300 mistresses.
6. These women turned his heart away from the Lord God of Israel.
7. In Solomon's old age, his heart was turned to worship the gods of his wives instead of being completely faithful to God.
8. He did what was evil in the sight of the Lord and refused to follow the Lord completely as his father David did.

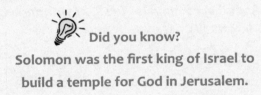

Did you know?
Solomon was the first king of Israel to
build a temple for God in Jerusalem.

Meditation
1. When you gave your life to Jesus Christ, you had been called into God's kingdom.
2. You had become light and should not be found in connection with any work of darkness.
3. As children of God, all of God's commands to guide our lives should be followed closely.
4. Solomon chose not to follow God's instructions and took the wrong path.
5. He joined himself with women that God told him not to and they drew him away from God.
6. When children of God are linked to people who are not on the

same path as them, they are distracted and not able to get to their destination.

7. As God's children, we should be careful of the type of friends we keep.

8. Any friend that will not help your relationship with God should be avoided.

9. You should be friends with those who will help you fulfil God's purpose for your life.

Reflection:
What type of friends
am I connected to?

Prayer
Dear Lord, please help me follow through with your
instructions and keep the right kind of friends
who will help me walk with you in Jesus' name. Amen

shine your Light

Bible Story: Acts 9:36-43 (Tabitha gave to the poor)

Memory Verse: Let your light so shine before men that they may see your good works and glorify your Father in heaven. (Matt 5:16 NKJV)

The Story

1. There was a believer in Joppa named Tabitha.

2. She was kind to others and helped the poor.

3. Then she became sick and died.

4. Her body was washed for burial and laid in an upstairs room.

5. The other believers heard that Apostle Peter was nearby at Lydda.

6. They sent two men to beg him to come as soon as possible.

7. Peter came with them, and they took him to the room where she was laid.

8. The room was filled with widows who were weeping and showing him the coats and clothes Tabitha had made for them.

9. Peter asked everyone to leave the room; then he knelt down to pray.

10. He turned to the body and said, 'Get up, Tabitha!'

11. She opened her eyes. When she saw Peter she sat up.

12. He gave her his hand and helped her up.

13. Peter called the widows and all believers and presented her to them alive.

14. The news spread throughout the whole town, and many believed in the Lord.

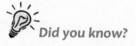
Did you know?

The Greek meaning of Tabitha is Dorcas.

Meditation

1. As a young believer, you are the light of the world.

2. God has blessed you so you can be a blessing to others.

3. That is how you can shine your light for the world to see.

4. Tabitha was a believer at Joppa, and she made an impact in the lives of others.

5. She died, but because she was a shining light by her kind deeds to the poor, the widows did not want her to die early.

6. When you shine your light as a Christian, you attract more people to you, and by that, you can share the gospel of Jesus with them.

7. We should not be Christians only by name or mere words, but it should show in our actions and behaviour.

8. Being a light means helping other people and showing them love.

9. This will make everyone know that we are children of God.

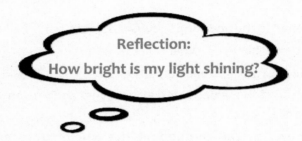

Reflection:

How bright is my light shining?

Prayer

Dear Father of light, I thank you for making me a light in this dark world. I pray for strength to keep my light shining for all to see in Jesus' name. Amen

Bible Story: Genesis 12:1-9 (The call of Abram)

Memory Verse: Your word is a lamp to my feet and a light to my path. (Psalm 119:105 NKJV)

The Story

1. God told Abram to leave his country and relatives and go to a different land that He would show him.

2. God gave him promises that He would bless him and make him famous.

3. Abram obeyed and left with his wife Sarai and nephew, Lot, and his belongings.

4. God told him again that He would give the Promised Land to his descendants.

5. Abram set up an altar and worshipped God.

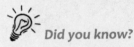 *Did you know?*

Abram was called when he was 75 years old.

Meditation

1. God's word served as a guide to Abram when he left the place he was familiar with.

2. As children of God, we cannot live our lives anyhow. We should live by the guidance of God.

3. We need to read God's word everyday to receive direction from Him. This will serve as a map and GPS to lead us in whatever we want to do.

4. We need to pray everyday, too, as God speaks back to us and leads us in prayer.

5. God's word can be received through some of these ways: (a) by reading the Bible directly, (b) using a daily devotional, (c) by listening to our Sunday school teachers and (d) through our parents at home.

6. No matter the way God's word comes to us, we should obey it.

7. God's word ensures that we live our lives in line with His plans and purposes for our lives.

8. God's word guarantees a successful arrival at our destination.

Reflection:
Are there times that I have not allowed God's word to serve as a compass for my life?

Prayer

Darling Saviour, I am grateful for the blessings of your word. Let me continue to be obedient to your word as it leads me and helps me get to where you want me to be in Jesus' name. Amen

Stand Fast in Faith

Bible Story: Numbers 13:1-33, 14:1-8 (Joshua and Caleb brought good report)

Memory Verse: Watch, stand fast in the faith, be brave, be strong. (1 Corinthians 16:13 NKJV)

The Story

1. God had promised the Israelites that He would give them Canaan, a land flowing with milk and honey.

2. God told Moses to send 12 men from the 12 tribes of Israel to go and explore Canaan.

3. He asked them to check whether the land was good or bad, whether the people were strong or weak, few or many, whether the land was rich or poor.

4. He also asked them to note the type of houses they lived in, the

type of trees they planted and many other demands.

5. He asked them to bring fruits from the land.

6. The men did as they were told. They came back after 40 days.

7. They brought with them bunches of grapes that they cut from the valley of Eshcol. They also brought fruits from both the pomegranate and fig trees.

8. They reported that the land was a good land flowing with milk and honey.

9. Ten of them said however, that the people were giants and were stronger than they were. They said the cities had large walls which they would not be able to climb or pull down.

10. Joshua and Caleb strongly believed that God would bring them into the land as a possession contrary to the report of the other spies.

Did you know?

The tribe of Levi did not go out to spy
because they were the priestly tribe.
Joseph became two tribes, Ephraim and Manasseh.

Meditation

1. God has given all His children the strength to overcome any battle or challenge they might face in life.

2. He wants us to believe that all things are possible for us if we have faith in Him.

3. Sometimes, certain situations may appear to be difficult for us to overcome. But we must always remember that there is nothing impossible for anyone that believes in God.

4. Usually, good things don't come cheap. They may come with some obstacles and challenges that need to be overcome.

5. Like Joshua and Caleb, we must focus on the good things that God has promised and be strong enough to get them. Commit the challenges to God, who can handle whatever we put into His hands.

6. As children of God, He has promised to give us a land flowing with milk and honey: a land that is fruitful and beautiful.

7. When situations arise that may shake our faith, we should rest on the promises of God, not wavering in faith, but being bold and full of courage like Joshua and Caleb.

Reflection:
How confident am I in God's promises for my life and family?

Prayer:
Lord, I know you have promised an abundance of
blessings for my family and me. But sometimes,
I become weak in my faith to get the blessings.
Now, Lord, I pray for increased faith to trust you and
strength to fight every challenge that may come my way.
Thank you, Father, in Jesus' Name I pray. Amen

Seek Godly Counsel

Bible Story: 1 kings 12:1-18 (Rehoboam picks the wrong counsel)

Memory verse: The way of fools seems right to them, but the wise listen to advice. (Proverbs 12:15 NKJV)

The Story

1. Rehoboam, the son of Solomon, went to Shechem, where the Israelites made him king.

2. When Jeroboam, the servant of Solomon, heard, he came back from Egypt.

43

3. He had escaped from King Solomon to Egypt.

4. Jeroboam and the Israelites went to speak to Rehoboam.

5. They told him that his father was a hard master and pleaded with Rehoboam to lighten the work and the heavy taxes he imposed on them. They promised to be loyal servants to him.

6. He told them to come back in 3 days for his answer.

7. Rehoboam asked the older counselors who counselled his father what their advice was.

8. The older counselors told him to give them a favourable answer and that they would serve him.

9. Rehoboam rejected their advice.

10. Rehoboam asked the young men who he had grown up with and who were now his advisers what he should do.

11. The young men told him to tell the people that his little finger was thicker than his father's waist.

12. That he would make their work heavier and beat them with scorpions instead of his father's whips.

13. When the people came back to hear his decision, he spoke harshly to them.

14. He had rejected the older men's advice and followed that of the young men.

15. All this was in line with the fulfilment of God's message.

16. The Israelites rejected Rehoboam as king and went back home.

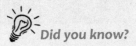 *Did you know?*

It was during the reign of Rehoboam
that Israel was split into two kingdoms.

Meditation

1. Life is a decision-making journey.
2. As a young Christian, you will be faced with situations that demand you to make a choice almost every day.
3. Sometimes, the choices will be easy to make on your own.
4. Some other times, you will need to ask for counsel.
5. You should always seek godly counsel and follow through with it when such situations arise.
6. Do not be like Rehoboam, who picked the counsel of the inexperienced young men and then lost the trust of his people.
7. Godly counsel gives us confidence.
8. When we follow godly counsel, it saves us from destruction.
9. When we make decisions, we should not do it in a hurry.
10. We should be patient and make the right choice.
11. Good counsel or advice will enable us to fulfil God's plan for our lives.

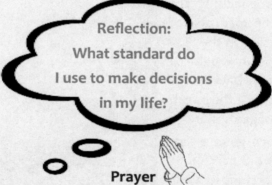

Reflection:
What standard do
I use to make decisions
in my life?

Prayer

Dear Father, I am always faced with a choice between so many pieces of advice that come from different groups of people. Please help me always to make the right decision in Jesus' name. Amen

Choose the Way of the Lord

Bible Story:1 Kings 13:1-25 (The young man of God and the Old Prophet)

Memory Verse: There is a way that seems right to a man, but its end is the way of death. (Proverbs 14:12 NKJV)

The Story

1. God commanded a man of God to go from Judah to Bethel.

2. As Jeroboam the king was approaching the altar, the man of God prophesied to the altar that Josiah would be born from David's clan and sacrifice the priests on the pagan's altar.

3. The Lord gave a sign that the altar would split apart, and its ashes poured on the ground.

4. When King Jeroboam heard the man of God speak, he pointed his

hand so that he could be seized, but instantly his hand became paralyzed. At the same time, a wide crack appeared in the altar and the ashes poured out.

5. The king cried that his hand be restored and the man of God prayed for him and his hand was restored.

6. The king asked the man of God to come to the palace so he could eat and get a gift from him.

7. The man of God declined and said that God commanded him not to eat or drink and not to go back the same way he came.

8. He left Bethel and went home another way.

9. There was an old prophet whose sons came back home and told him all that the man of God from Judah had done.

10. The old prophet asked which way the man of God went and he followed him after his sons had saddled his donkey for him.

11. He met the man of God sitting under a great tree.

12. The old prophet confirmed his identity and asked that he

47

should come home with him to eat some food.

13. He first declined and told the old prophet that God had said he should not eat, drink, or go back home the same way he came.

14. But the old prophet convinced him by saying that he too was a prophet and that an angel had commanded him to bring the man of God home so he could eat and drink, but the old prophet was lying to him.

15. While they were eating at the table, the old prophet received a command from God and declared that since the man of God had defied the word of the Lord and disobeyed, his body would not be buried in the grave of his ancestors.

16. Afterwards, the man of God saddled his donkey and started his journey.

17. As he was travelling along, a lion came out and killed him and it stood beside his corpse.

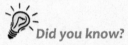 *Did you know?*

Jeroboam was the worst king Israel ever had
because no king was able to totally get
rid of the sins that he made Israel commit.

Meditation

1. The young man of God was commanded by God to go to Judah and speak against the altar upon which Jeroboam had been burning a strange fire.

2. He heeded the call but did not follow through with the other instructions that God gave him.

3. He was deceived by the old prophet because his words were juicy and sweet.

4. He lied that an angel had given a different instruction.

5. Whenever God gives us instructions, we should hold on to them and follow them to the letter.

6. Until we have carried out the instruction, we are not permitted to take a break.

7. Sometimes, a way may seem right to us, but the way may be the way to destruction.

8. When we hear two voices make suggestions to us, we must choose to listen to the voice of God, which leads to life.

9. We must then do what the voice of God commands us to do, not what the other person claims to "hear" from God.

10. God's voice will never lead us to a bad end.

Reflection:

Whose way should I choose?

Prayer

Dear Father, sometimes, my ways seem right to me, but they may end in destruction. Help me to trust your decision and follow your ways in Jesus' name. Amen

o b e y
Immediately

Bible Story: Genesis 6:5-22 (The Story of Noah)

Memory Verse: Then I heard the voice of the Lord saying, "whom shall I send, and who will go for us?" And I said, "Here am I, Send me!" (Isaiah 6:8 NIV)

The Story

1. The Lord saw that humans had become very wicked.

2. He became sorry to have created man and wanted a fresh start.

3. He decided to wipe out the whole creation on earth.

4. He found Noah and his family clean and without fault.

5. Noah's sons were Shem, Ham, and Japheth.

6. God commanded Noah to build an ark with specific instructions.

7. He commanded Noah to bring every living creature into the ark: male and female.

8. God was ready to destroy the earth with water.

9. Noah did everything just as God commanded him.

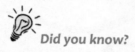

Did you know?

Only eight people made it to the ark and
started the new world after the flood.

Meditation:

1. Many times in our day-to-day living, we read God's word and also hear it.

2. Obedience is an essential expectation that God has of you.

3. Obedience must be immediate.

4. Following instructions must be done right away.

5. When our parents, teachers and others who have guardianship over us give us instructions to carry out, we should not delay.

6. According to a songwriter, "Action is the key, do it immediately."

7. One of the reasons why we should not delay is that we might change our minds altogether and eventually disobey the instructions given.

8. Delay may also make us lose sight of some necessary details we might have been given.

9. When you obey promptly, both the one who gives instructions and the one who carries out the instructions have joy.

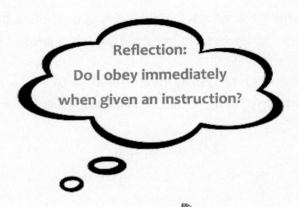

Reflection:
Do I obey immediately
when given an instruction?

Prayer
Gracious Father, I know obedience is vital in walking with you; help me act on instructions immediately without delay, in Jesus' name. Amen

Study 14 — obey completely

Bible story: 1 Samuel 15: 1-15 (Saul and the destruction of the Amalekites)

Memory Verse: To obey is better than sacrifice, and to heed is better than the fat of rams. (1 Samuel 15:22b NIV)

The Story

1. Samuel the prophet went to Saul the king to give him a message from the LORD.

2. God wanted to judge the nation of Amalek for opposing Israel when they came out of Egypt.

3. God commanded Israel through Saul to completely destroy the entire Amalekite nation.

4. Saul immediately got the army ready: 200,000 soldiers from Israel and 10,000 men from Judah.

5. Saul sent a message to the Kenites that they should move away from the nation of Amalek so that they would not be destroyed with them. This was because the Kenites showed kindness to the people of Israel when they left Egypt for the Promised Land.

6. Saul and his army completely destroyed everyone and everything else, but he captured King Agag alive and kept the best of the sheep, goats, cattle, calves and lambs and everything that appealed to him.

7. He destroyed only the things that were worthless and of poor quality.

8. The LORD told Samuel that since Saul refused to completely obey all that He commanded him, He was sorry that He made him king. Samuel cried to God all night for Saul.

9. Samuel looked for Saul the following day.

10. With excitement, Saul greeted Samuel and told him he had carried out the LORD's command.

11. Samuel challenged him that he heard the bleating of sheep, goats, and cattle in his compound.

12. Saul admitted later that he kept the best of the sheep and oxen to sacrifice to the LORD but destroyed every other thing.

13. Saul gave Samuel the word from God that as a leader, the LORD expected him to obey His word totally, but he kept back those things that appealed to him.

14. Saul argued that he had obeyed the LORD.

15. Samuel said 'Until obedience is complete, it is not obedience.'

16. As a result, God rejected Saul as king.

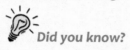
Did you know?

Saul was the first King of Israel.

Meditations

1. In our previous study, we understood that part of God's expectations of you is prompt obedience. This means doing what He commands you immediately.

2. The other side of the coin is not just obeying immediately, but also obeying everything God commands you to do.

3. You may be tempted to consider yourself very brilliant when you score 9 out of 10, which is considered excellent for school grading. With obedience, 9 out of 10 could be regarded as disobedience.

4. Obedience should be 100% all the time. Whenever you receive instructions from God, your teachers, parents, pastors, or those who have authority over you, they should be carried out immediately and totally.

5. No part of the instruction should be left out. It may not be easy, but as you ask God for help, He will give you all you need to get to that level of fully committing to Him.

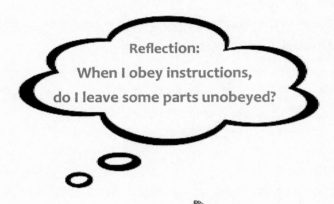

Reflection:

When I obey instructions,

do I leave some parts unobeyed?

Prayer

Dear LORD, when you give me instructions to carry out, please help me follow them step by step without leaving out any part. Thank you, LORD, for giving me the grace in Jesus' name. Amen

Obey with all your Heart

Bible Story: 2 Chronicles 25:1-2 (King Amaziah did not obey God with his whole heart)

Memory Verse: You shall love the Lord your God with all your heart, with all your soul, and with all your strength. (Deuteronomy 6:5 NKJV)

The Story

1. Amaziah was one of the sons of Joash.

2. He became a king after his father died.
3. He was 25 years old when his reign began.

4. He did what was pleasing and correct in the eyes of the LORD.
5. But he did not do it with his whole heart.

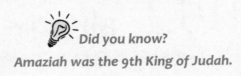

Did you know?

Amaziah was the 9th King of Judah.

Meditation

1. Obeying immediately and totally are key expectations of God from you.
2. He wants obedience to be done with all your heart.
3. Sometimes, we obey so we do not face the consequences of disobedience.
4. God is asking for obedience that comes with no complaint or murmur.
5. You should remember that God sees the heart and judges our actions based on our motives which no one but only Him sees.
6. Who could have thought that despite all that Amaziah did that was pleasing to God, it was not with his whole heart?
7. He did not really want to obey God. He probably did it only because he was mandated to do it. He did it reluctantly.
8. As a young Christian, it is not strange to find yourself in a situation like this from time to time but what you can do is to go back to God and make your heart right.
9. Repent and tell Him to help you so that your obedience will be from a heart that really wants to obey God.

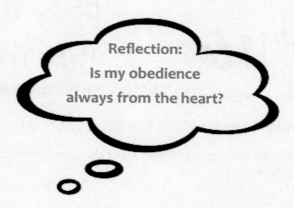

Reflection:
Is my obedience
always from the heart?

Prayer

**Dear Lord, you know I sincerely love you and my parents
and will always love to obey with a perfect heart. Help me,
Lord, to always have a right heart in Jesus' name. Amen**

Obey all the Time

Bible Story: Joshua 6:1-20 (The fall of Jericho)

Memory Verse: You are my friends if you do what I command.
(John 15:14 NLT)

The Story

1. Jericho was a great city surrounded by a wall, but the people there were afraid of the Israelites who surrounded them. So, they did not allow anybody to go out or come into the city.

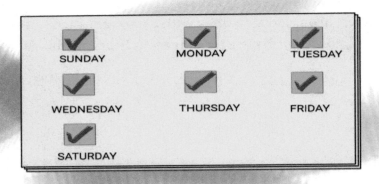

2. This was because the people of Jericho knew that the Israelites would soon conquer them.

3. The Lord gave the Israelites stepwise instructions to follow through Joshua, their leader.

4. They were to march around the city wall once a day for six days.

5. Seven priests were to walk ahead of the ark, each carrying a ram's horn.

6. They were to march around the city wall seven times on the seventh day.

7. Once they heard the blast of the ram's horns, the people were instructed to shout as loud as they could.

8. But the people were to remain silent until they were told to shout.

9. They were told that the city walls would fall flat after they shout.

10. The priests and the people of Israel did exactly as God commanded them.

11. God also told them to completely destroy everything except Rahab, the prostitute. Her household and all that she had were spared because she protected the spies sent by Joshua to Jericho earlier on.

12. But everything made from silver, gold, bronze, or iron was to be brought to the treasury as sacred to the LORD.

 *Did you know?*

The walls of Jericho were about 4 meters tall.

Meditation:

1. Obedience is a lifelong journey.

2. When you became a Christian, you signed up for a lifetime journey of immediate, complete, wholehearted and consistent obedience.

3. The children of Israel in this story had to obey specific instructions for seven days without missing a day.

4. Imagine them carrying out the instruction the first six days and ignoring it on the 7th day; what would be the outcome? Would the walls of Jericho still fall flat? NO!

5 Therefore, to live daily as children of God and get the expected results, you have to demonstrate unfailing obedience.

6 Obedience must be done steadily, consistently, and always as we walk with God.

7 The Israelites knew that for them to get Jericho as theirs as God had promised, they had to follow through on their obedience to the given instructions.

8 The same thing applies to you as a young Christian that to get all the promises of our heavenly Father and get to the Promised Land, you need to obey every second, every minute, every hour and every day.

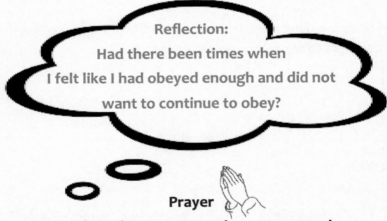

Reflection:
Had there been times when
I felt like I had obeyed enough and did not
want to continue to obey?

Prayer

Heavenly Father, I want to obey you every day.

Sometimes I try so hard but I still fail. Help me to follow through on the instructions you have given me consistently in Jesus' name. Amen

I Can do all Things through Christ

Bible Story: Daniel 2:1-24 (Daniel interprets the dream of Nebuchadnezzar)

Memory Verse: I can do all things through Christ that strengthens me. (Philippians 4:13 NKJV)

The Story

1. Nebuchadnezzar had a dream that gave him a sleepless night.

2. The king called the magicians to tell him his dream because he could not remember.

3. He wanted the interpretation too.

4. The magicians told the king that it was impossible.

5. Daniel was listed as one of the wise men in Babylon.

6. Daniel and his Hebrew friends asked God to reveal the dream and its interpretation to them.

7. God answered their request.

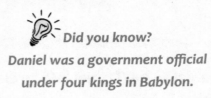

Did you know?

Daniel was a government official under four kings in Babylon.

Meditation

1. Each new grade in school comes with its own challenges.

2. The subjects usually get tougher and more demanding.

3. Sometimes, it is not easy to understand what the teacher is saying but remember the memory verse of today that Jesus Christ has given us the strength to do all things.

4. Like Daniel and his friends, he expects you to ask Him for help.

5. After doing your part by working hard, you can achieve your dreams and aspirations in life if you ask God for help.

6. No matter how challenging the subjects are, you can do well in them with God's help.

7. Depending on His strength shows that you totally trust Him.

Reflection:

In what areas do I need

God to help me?

Prayer

Dear Lord, I ask that you help me today with my
difficult tasks and classwork. Thank you, Jesus, because
I can do all things through you, who gives me strength.
I pray for my classmates that are struggling.
Please help them too, in Jesus' name. Amen

I am Secure in Jesus

Bible Story: Matthew 8:23-27 (Jesus calmed the storm)

Memory Verse: For ye are dead, and your life is hid with Christ in God. (Colossians 3:3 KJV)

The Story

1. Jesus got into the boat with His disciples.

2. A fierce storm struck and broke the boat.

3. Jesus was sleeping at the back of the boat.

4. One of the disciples woke Him up shouting, 'Lord save us! We're going to drown.'

5. Jesus asked them, 'Why are you afraid? You have so little faith!'

6. Jesus got up and rebuked the wind and waves. Suddenly, there was a great calm.

7. The disciples were amazed that the winds and waves obeyed him.

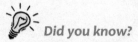 *Did you know?*

Both living and non-living things can obey God's word.

Meditation

1. The world is full of fierce storms that can be likened to diseases, sicknesses, and different types of trouble.

2. We should always be reminded that Jesus is in the storm with us.

3. It may look like He is sometimes sleeping, but He is aware of our troubles.

4. Just a word from Him can bring the solutions to the questions of our lives.

5. Just a gesture can calm the storms and the raging seas troubling our lives.

6. We have to believe in Him and show that we have faith even as tiny as a small grain.

7. We should always remember that we are secure in Him even though the world may be shaking.

Reflection:
How secure do I feel in Him?

Prayer

Heavenly Father, there are a lot of ups and downs in the world today. Troubles on every side, plagues and illnesses are ravaging the world. Lord, in the middle of this, let me feel secure and safe in you. I pray for those who are experiencing different types of troubles that you will deliver them from such in Jesus' name. Amen

Bible Story: Mark 14:66-72; Acts 2:14-18 (Peter denied Jesus but later preached the gospel with boldness with the help of the Holy Spirit)

Memory Verse: So, we may boldly say: The Lord is my helper; I will not fear. What can man do to me? (Hebrews 13:6 NKJV)

The Story

1. After Jesus had been led away to the high priest, Peter followed Him at a distance.

2. Peter was warming himself at the fire in the courtyard when a servant girl looked at Peter and said, 'You also were with Jesus', but he said NO.

3. The servant girl saw him standing, and she told others that Peter was for sure one of the disciples.

4. He went outside, and then some people told him again, 'You are

one of the disciples by the way you speak,' but he said NO again.

5. Immediately the rooster crowed, Peter remembered the words of Jesus, that he would deny Him three times before the cock crowed and he cried.

6. Before His ascension, Jesus told His disciples to wait for the Holy Spirit that He would send.

7. After the ascension of Jesus, the disciples assembled in a place to pray and wait for the baptism of the Holy Spirit.

8. Suddenly they heard a sound like a mighty wind from heaven that filled the house.

9. Like a tongue of fire, the Holy Spirit rested upon each one of them.

10. As a result, they began to speak in different languages.

11. After the Pentecost experience, the crowd made fun of Peter and the disciples and said that they were probably drunk because they spoke in new languages.

12. Peter stood in front of the crowd and preached the gospel of Jesus Christ with boldness under the power of the Holy Spirit.

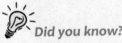

Did you know?

The Holy Spirit can make a timid person bold.

Meditation

1. Peter was one of the closest disciples to Jesus.

2. He truly loved Jesus, to the extent that when he was arrested in Gethsemane, all the disciples left him but Peter watched from afar.

3. He was timid and denied Jesus when a little girl that identified

him as one of the disciples of Jesus Christ confronted him.

4. But in the Book of Acts when the Holy Spirit came and rested upon every disciple, including Peter, he became bold.

5. As young Christians after we have given our lives to Jesus Christ, we need the baptism of the Holy Spirit.

6. It is through the help of the Holy Spirit that our Christian journey can be easy.

7. He is the third personality of the Godhead and the one that Jesus left with us when he went back to heaven.

8. We should ask for the baptism of the Holy Spirit as soon as we become born again.

9. After Peter had received the Holy Spirit, he was able to stand in front of a large crowd and witness Jesus to them.

10. As children, sometimes we are timid or fearful, but the presence of the Holy Spirit in us brings us the Spirit of boldness.

11. We can face our giants with confidence when the Holy Spirit dwells in us.

12. The Holy Spirit teaches us all things. He also leads us in the way to go.

Reflection:
What or who am I afraid of?

Prayer

Holy Spirit, I reject every Spirit of fear and timidity, and I receive the Spirit of boldness and courage. I pray that every child experiencing fear be delivered in Jesus' name. Amen

Living for Jesus

Bible Story: Daniel 6:1-20 (Daniel prayed three times a day)

Memory Verse: But clothe yourself with the Lord Jesus Christ and forget about satisfying your sinful self. (Romans 13:14 NCV)

The Story

1. King Darius divided his kingdom into 120 provinces and appointed officers.

2. He chose Daniel and two others to supervise the officers and protect the king's interest.

3. Daniel proved himself more capable.

4. The king planned to place him over the whole empire.

5. The other officers were jealous. They looked for some fault in Daniel but could not find any.

6. He was faithful, responsible, and completely trustworthy.

7. They concluded they could only accuse him based on the law of his religion.

8. All the other officials went to meet the king and advised him to make a law that anybody who would bow or worship any god or man for thirty days, apart from the king should be thrown into the den of lions.

9. Daniel did not obey the king because he prayed three times a day to the God of Israel, his God.

10. He was arrested and brought to the king for disobeying him.

11. Daniel was cast into the den of lions.

12. The lions did not hurt him.

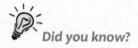 *Did you know?*

Daniel's Babylonian name is Belteshazzar.

Meditation

1. Daniel chose to live his life so that no one could accuse him of any wrongdoing.

2. As young believers, God expects that we live a life that is void of errors or bad character.

3. It is impressive that the only way they could trap or get Daniel in trouble was by his devotion to his God.

4. We are challenged that we should live for Jesus in every moment.

5. We should strive to live lives free of errors or wrongdoing.

6. Even if the expression of our faith and belief gets us in trouble, we should remember that God will miraculously get us out of it as he did for Daniel.

7. He loves it when we are proud of him and of our faith.

8. We should not only profess or confess that we are Christians, but we should also show it by our lifestyle.

9. Our relationship with others, work style, school life, etc., should show that we are living for Jesus.

10. Simple acts like praying on our food before we eat lunch, not just in private but also in public, praying with someone who asks us for help etc., can show that we are living for Jesus.

11. When we choose to live for Jesus, it will show in everything we do and those that are around us will see it and give glory to our God.

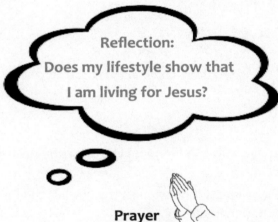

Reflection:
Does my lifestyle show that
I am living for Jesus?

Prayer

Lord Jesus, help me to live for you day by day without any wrongdoing. I pray for every young Christian like me who may be struggling to live for Jesus, let the Holy Spirit make it easy for us in Jesus' name. Amen

By God, I am made strong

Bible Story: Judges 6:1-22 (Gideon strengthened by God to lead)

Memory Verse: The Lord is my light and my salvation, whom shall I fear, the Lord is the strength of my life, of whom shall I be afraid? (Psalm 27:1 NKJV)

The Story

1. Israel did evil in the sight of God, so God made them servants to the Midianites for 7 years.

2. Then the Israelites cried out to God for help.

3. God sent them a prophet to tell them to worship Him, but they did not listen.

4. Then the angel of the Lord was sent to Gideon, who was from the tribe of Manasseh and the least in his family.

5. The angel told him to go and deliver his people with the strength God had given him.

6. Gideon asked for a sign.

7. He cooked a young goat and brought it to the angel. The angel touched it with the tip of his staff, and fire came upon the cooked goat.

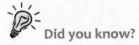 Did you know?

Gideon was one of the greatest of the

fifteen Judges that ruled in Israel.

Meditation

1. Sometimes in life, we may be faced with many challenges.

2. Some of them are caused by our disobedience or sins.

3. Sometimes, things just happen regardless of what we do or what we do not do.

4. Also, we might be given assignments that look bigger than our age or abilities.

5. When we are in such positions, we can always ask God for help by praying to Him and He will be willing to help us out.

6. Even if we are not confident that He can help us, He is still willing to work with us every step along the way until that confidence is developed.

7. He can increase our level of trust in Him.

8. His strength gets rid of our fears.

9. It is in His strength that we are made strong.

10. We can therefore be able to accomplish much because we have been made strong by God.

Reflection:
What are my fears?

Prayer

Dear Lord, I am sorry for my disobedience and sins that might have led me to this challenging situation. Save me, Lord, and remove every fear from me. Please give me the strength that I need to accomplish the task that is ahead of me. I pray also for my friends that are weak that you will give them your strength in Jesus' name. Amen

God will always Provide

Bible Story: (1 Kings 17:2-9) Elijah was fed by the ravens

Memory Verse: And my God shall supply all your need according to His riches in glory by Christ Jesus. (Philippians 4:19 NKJV)

The Story

1. There was a famine in the land of Israel.

2. The Lord told Elijah to go to the East and hide by the brook Kerith near River Jordan.

3. The Lord told him to drink from the brook and eat what the ravens bring to him.

4. God had commanded the ravens to bring him food.

5. Elijah did what God told him.

6. The ravens brought him bread and meat every morning and evening.

7. After some time, the brook dried up because there was no rain.

8. God then told Elijah to go and live in a village called Zarephath near Sidon.

9. God had told a widow to feed Elijah.

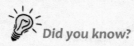 *Did you know?*

Ravens are big birds that feed mainly on meat.

Meditation

1. The Lord has promised that all our needs will be met as we trust Him and follow His commandments.

2. Despite the famine in the land, God sent provision of food and water to Elijah.

3. Even though ravens are big birds that feed mainly on meat, God used the ravens to bring bread and meat to Elijah twice a day.

4. It is God's promise for us that regardless of what is happening around us and in the world, He can and will provide for all our needs.

5. As long as we obey His instructions and listen to Him, He is ready to step into the most difficult situations and give us a breakthrough.

6. When brook Kerith dried up, God had another provision ready for Elijah.

7. As children of God, our father in heaven will not let us beg for bread at any stage of our lives. What we need is to listen to Him and do what He commands us to do.

8. Our provision is sure when we remain in Him.

Reflection:
Do I trust God to provide
for me and my family?

Prayer

Father, I thank you for always providing for me.
Please continue to supply my needs and those of my
family so that we will lack nothing. I also pray
that there will be provision for those in need
in Jesus' name. Amen

God Fights for His People

Bible Story: Judges 7:1-22 (Few of Gideon's army were used to defeat the Midianites)

Memory Verse: For nothing restrains the Lord from saving by many or by few. (I Samuel 14: 6b, NIV)

The Story

1. God had called Gideon to deliver the children of Israel from the Midianites.

2. Lots of Gideon's men were interested in fighting the battle, thirty-two thousand of them but God told Gideon that they were too many.

3. God told him to announce to the men that whoever was afraid should go back home.

4. Twenty-two thousand men were afraid and went back home.

5. Ten thousand of them remained, but God said they were still too many.

6. God told Gideon to take them down to the water to drink.

7. The ten thousand soldiers were divided into two groups– those who knelt to drink water and those who stood up and lapped the water with their tongues like dogs.

8. Three hundred men had stood up and lapped the water from their hands while the remaining men knelt to drink water.

9. God told Gideon that he would use only three hundred men to give Israel victory in the battle and the others were sent back home.

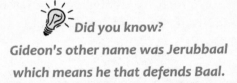 *Did you know?*

Gideon's other name was Jerubbaal
which means he that defends Baal.

Meditation

1. As humans, sometimes we feel that going to the best schools, living in the best neighbourhoods, being raised in a developed country, or having wealthy parents and so many other rare privileges is all we need to be successful in life.

2. As good as all these seem to be, they are not the primary keys to success.

3. God was trying to teach Gideon a lesson of total dependence on Him in the battle he had to fight.

4. Only God can guarantee us success in every phase of our lives.

5. The charge for us as children of God is to totally depend on God and obey what he tells us in order to attain the success we so desire.

6. He expects us to play our own part and leave the rest to Him to play His own.

7. We should always make Him our strength in all that we do.

8. We should never depend only on physical things for our success because things may change suddenly.

9. Our total trust should be in God and only this will guarantee us the success we want.

Reflection:

Do I depend on God totally especially when things are already working?

Prayer

Dear Lord, I thank you for the blessings of my family, a safe place to live in, and all those good things that you have surrounded me with. Father, please give me the grace to always trust you and your word for good success in my life's journey in Jesus' name. Amen

Fighting Spiritual Wars

Bible Story: Daniel 10:7-14 (God's answers to Daniel's prayers were withstood)

Memory Verse: For we do not wrestle against flesh and blood but against principalities, against powers, against the rulers of the darkness of this age, against spiritual hosts of wickedness in the heavenly places. (Ephesians 6:12 NKJV)

The Story

1. Daniel alone saw a vision that others around him did not see.
2. He became weak and looked pale.

3. A true message was revealed to Daniel about future events.
4. Daniel had been fasting for 21 days.

5. Only Daniel saw the vision, which made him lay face to the ground.

6. An angel told Daniel that his prayers were heard in heaven the same day he prayed but the answer was blocked by spiritual forces in Persia for 21 days.

7. Archangel Michael, one of the chief angels, came to help the messenger angel to let the answer get to Daniel eventually.

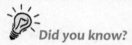

Did you know?

Gabriel was the messenger angel

(an archangel) that brought Daniel's answers.

Meditation

1. The world is a spiritual battlefield.

2. Everything we see physically is dictated by the spiritual realms.

3. If God should open our eyes to the spiritual realm, we will see that we are fighting spiritual wars daily.

4. The fact that we are children does not exempt us from these wars.

5. Prayer is an essential tool and weapon for all Christians to fight these wars.

6. Prayer allows us to lay claim to things that rightfully belong to us.

7. Warfare prayers make us put an end to any bad trend that we may be seeing manifesting in the physical realm around us.

8. As believers, it is important to know that when we are fighting a spiritual battle there may be barriers but with consistent prayers, answers will surely come.

9. There are different types of prayers.

(a) There is the prayer of thanksgiving whereby you give thanks to God for what he has done and what he will do.

(b) There is the prayer of adoration where you hallow God for who He is.

(c) There is the prayer of supplication where you ask God for specific needs to be met and

(d) There is the prayer of intercession, where you pray for other people.

10. When things are going the right way, we should pray.

11. When things are going the wrong way, we should pray.

12. Prayer is hard work and not child's play.

13. Grace and strength are available to us as we pray.

14. We should use all the weapons we have been given to fight. Some of them are:

(a) The blood of Jesus

(b) The word of God

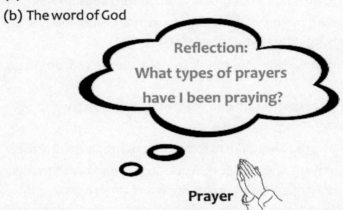

Reflection:

What types of prayers

have I been praying?

Prayer

The God of angel armies, I believe you are ready to answer all my prayers. Therefore, I come against any hindrance to my prayers right now, and I receive total victory in Jesus' name. Amen

Forgive One Another

Bible Story: Matthew 18:21-25 (The parable of the unforgiving servant)

Memory Verse: And be ye kind one to another, tender-hearted, forgiving one another, even as God for Christ's sake hath forgiven you. (Ephesians 4:32 NKJV)

The Story

1. A king wanted to bring his accounts up to date with his servants.

2. One of the servants owed a lot of money and could not pay it back. The king ordered that everyone and everything the servant had should be sold so he could repay.

3. The servant begged, and the king pitied him, then forgave him of the debt.

4. That same servant went and found a fellow servant who owed him a tiny amount of money and demanded instant payment.

5. The fellow servant begged for a little more time to pay, but he disagreed. Instead, he got him arrested and put him in prison.

6. The other servants were upset and reported him to the king.

7. The king called him evil because he was forgiven a lot, but he could not forgive his fellow servant a little.

Did you know that?

Jesus wants us to forgive one another

just as God has forgiven us.

Meditation

1. God has planted us into families and surrounded us with beautiful friends and neighbours.

2. Sometimes we tend to step on each other's toes.

3. There will sometimes be disagreements, minor fights, and many annoying statements that our family members, friends and neighbours may say.

4. It may be hard to forgive such people, especially if those offences have made us feel hurt and angry.

5. Each time this happens, it is good to remember that because Christ forgave us, we should find it necessary to forgive everyone who has hurt us, notwithstanding what they do or have done to us.

6. The Lord's Prayer says forgive us our sins as we forgive those who sin against us.

7. So, it follows that our forgiveness by God is based on forgiving other people who hurt us.

8. We also might have hurt people at some point in our lives; we should ask such people for forgiveness as well.

9. If the world has many forgivers, the world will be a better place to live in.

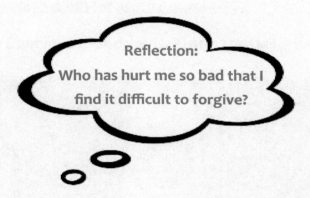

Reflection:
Who has hurt me so bad that I
find it difficult to forgive?

Prayer

Heavenly Father, I know that sometimes my friends and family members hurt me. My siblings and friends also deliberately do lots of annoying things. Lord, I ask that you help me find it easy to forgive them, knowing fully well that you have forgiven me my past sins and you will forgive me sins that I may commit each time I ask for forgiveness in Jesus' name. Amen

You will be Preferred

Bible Story: Esther 2:1-18 (Esther chosen as queen)

Memory Verse: You have loved righteousness and hated lawlessness. Therefore, God, your God, has anointed you with the oil of gladness more than your companions. (Hebrews 1:9 NKJV)

The Story

1. The anger of King Xerxes went down after he had thought about what Vashti (the former queen) did to him.

2. His personal attendants suggested that the king search the

empire for beautiful virgin girls and choose one who would please the king the most.

3. The chosen virgin would then be the next queen. The king was satisfied with the suggestion.

4. Mordecai lived around the king's palace and had a cousin called Esther, whom he had adopted because she was an orphan.

5. Esther and other girls were put in Hegai's (the king's servant) care.

6. Mordecai and many other Jews were moved from Jerusalem to Babylon by King Nebuchadnezzar.

7. Esther found favour before Hegai, and he treated her specially.

8. Mordecai had instructed Esther not to tell anyone about her nationality or family background.

9. Mordecai checked on Esther from a distance every day to ensure she was alright.

10. The girls were given beauty treatment for one year before meeting the king.

11. The king would only call on the virgin again if he wanted her as the queen.

12. Esther followed the guidance of the palace officials. She was admired by everyone who saw her.

13. The king made her the queen. Her uncle was also made one of the palace officials.

14. She continued to obey Mordecai even after she became the queen.

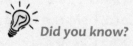 *Did you know?*

Esther's Jewish name was Hadassah.

Meditation

1. Even though Esther was an orphan, she obeyed her cousin, whom she stayed with.

2. Her obedience led her to get to the palace. Not only that, but she also became the queen of the entire province instead of Vashti.

3. As children we are encouraged to obey our parents, guardians, and those who have authority over us as long as they lead us in the Lord's way.

4. Obedience and loving righteousness brings favour and the grace to be the most preferred among colleagues and mates.

5. As children of God, loving God's way and disliking sin makes us stand out and be preferred among our mates.

6. It puts us in line for promotion and lifting.

7. Following God's ways and doing the right things make us excel in life.

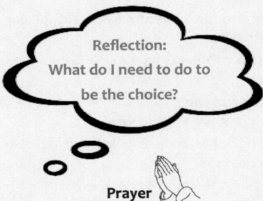

Reflection:
What do I need to do to
be the choice?

Prayer

Lord, obedience helped Esther to be anointed and crowned above her mates. Lord, help me to be obedient and preferred everywhere I get to in Jesus' name. Amen

Bible Story: Genesis 4:1-12 (The story of Cain and Abel)

Memory Verse: Whatever your hand finds to do, do it with all your might. (Ecclesiastes chapter 9:10a NIV)

The Story

1. Cain was the first born of Adam and Eve.

2. Cain had a brother called Abel.

3. Abel was a shepherd boy, but Cain was a farmer.

4. Both of them brought offerings to the LORD.

5. Abel gave God the best part of what he had.

6. God was pleased with Abel's offering but was displeased with Cain's because he did not give his best.

7. Cain was furious. Out of jealousy, he deceived his brother to the field and killed him. God cursed Cain for what he did.

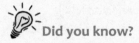 Did you know?

Cain was the first murderer (the first person to kill someone because he planned to) in the Bible.

Meditation

1. As young Christians, God has a high expectation of us, just like our parents at home, teachers at school, the government, and the world.

2. There is a list of what these people expect from us, which is also applicable to God. He made us and therefore, it is natural and expected that He has expectations of us.

3. What God wants from us is that we give everything we do our best shot.

4. From the story of Cain and Abel, the difference between their offerings was that Abel gave the best of what he had. (Adam and Eve must have taught their boys that God demanded an offering that was the best they could give).

5. Cain decided to approach God his way. He thought he knew better.

6. As a young Christian, we must always put in our best in our fellowship with God, our schoolwork, the home chores assigned to us, and anything that may be committed into our hands.

7. We should not disappoint or frustrate God regarding His expectation of us.

8. When we give our best shot to our schoolwork, assignments, preparation for examinations, and everything required of us, we expect outstanding results.

9. Giving everything our best shot pleases God, our parents and ourselves.

Reflection:
How often do I give my best
shot in things I do?

Prayer

Dear Lord, I always want to do my best as expected of me. Please give me the grace and strength to always give it my best every day and every time in Jesus' name. Amen

Bible Story: Luke 17:11-19 (Ten lepers were healed)

Memory Verse: In everything, give thanks, for this is the will of God in Christ Jesus for you. (1 Thessalonians 5:18 NKJV)

The Story

1. Jesus was going to Jerusalem when ten men who had a terrible contagious skin disease called leprosy cried out to Him, saying, "have mercy on us". They wanted him to heal them of their disease.

2. Jesus gave them instructions to go and show themselves to the priest according to the custom of the Jews.

3. On their way, one of them saw that he was healed and came back to Jesus to thank Him.

4. This man was a Samaritan.

5. Jesus asked for the other nine men.

6. Jesus told him that he was perfectly healed and made whole because he came back to say thank you.

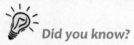 *Did you know?*

Jesus healed everyone that asked him for healing.

Meditation

1. Giving thanks should be the lifestyle of every Christian.

2. We should not wait only to give thanks on National Thanksgiving Day when we have prepared turkey and other food types.

3. When we give thanks to God continually, He will double our blessings and do more for us in the future.

4. We should not be too excited when we receive answers to prayers and then forget to say thank you to the Lord.

5. There is a saying that a thoughtful heart is a thankful heart.

6. There are many things that we can be thankful for.

7. Sometimes, the things we take for granted are things that some people are praying to have.

8. Can you cultivate a habit to always give thanks?

9. As young Christians, we should develop a lifestyle of saying thank you to God daily for His many blessings in our lives.

10. We should also thank people who help us or give us gifts.

11. It is always a good thing to give thanks all the time.

Reflection:
Do I always give thanks to
God for His many blessings
I enjoy every day?

Prayer

Dear Lord, I look back at all the great and
wonderful things you have done for my family and me.
I have come back to say thank you. I am sorry for not
thanking you enough when my prayers are answered.
Father, forgive me for being ungrateful in Jesus' name.
Amen

Unusual Obedience

Bible Story: Genesis 22:1-18 (Abraham sacrificing Isaac)

Memory Verse: If you are willing and obedient, you will eat the good things of the land. (Isaiah 1:19 NKJV)

The Story

1. After some time that Abraham had received the promise of a son by the name Isaac, God asked him to sacrifice that son as a burnt offering on a mountain in the land of Moriah.

2. The next day, Abraham got up early in the morning, got his donkey ready and took two servants and his son Isaac with him.

3. He got the wood ready and set out on the journey.

4. On the third day, when he saw the place from afar, he left the donkey with the servants and told them he and Isaac would go to worship and would be right back.

5. Isaac carried the wood while Abraham carried the fire and the knife.

6. After a while, Isaac asked his father where the sheep for the burnt offering was since they had the other materials.

7. Abraham answered him that the Lord would provide.

8. Abraham built an altar when they got to the place. He arranged the wood on it and then tied his son Isaac and laid him on top of the wood. Isaac never complained.

9. Immediately, the angel of the Lord called Abraham and told him not to hurt the boy.

10. By choosing to fear the Lord and obey what he was told, Abraham passed the test of unusual and complete obedience.

11. Abraham looked and saw a ram he sacrificed instead of his son.

12. God promised to bless him and multiply his descendants because he passed the test.

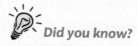 *Did you know?*

It was on the same mountain in Moriah

where Abraham wanted to sacrifice

Isaac that Jesus was crucified.

Meditation

1. Many times the instructions we may receive from God are straightforward and easy to relate to.

2. At some odd times however, what He may instruct us to do may be strange and unusual.

3. When we trust Him just like Abraham, we will know that He has our best interest at heart even when those unusual instructions are given.

4. Like Abraham of old, sacrificing Isaac was asking far too much and seemed unexpected and impossible.

5. God did this as a test before Abraham could go to his next level of blessings.

6. As a young Christian, God might be asking us to do strange things like leaving our place of comfort and going to a far land to preach the gospel. He may ask us to do things that look too big for a young Christian.

7. As we improve and invest in our relationship with God and take time to know Him more by reading His word and praying, certain things will begin to happen to us.

8. We will develop trust, recognize his voice when he speaks, and we will increase in faith to follow through with any instruction He may give us, no matter how strange or unusual it looks.

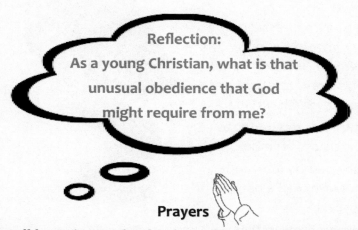

Reflection:
As a young Christian, what is that unusual obedience that God might require from me?

Prayers

The all-knowing God, I thank you because you are a Father I can trust. Therefore, whenever you give me instructions, help me follow through even though they might sound strange in Jesus' name. Amen

Study 30

I need Timely Help from God

Bible Story: Genesis 21:8-20 (Hagar and Ishmael were provided with water)

Memory Verse: I will lift up my eyes to the hills, from where comes my help, my help comes from the Lord who makes heaven and earth.
(Psalm 121:1, 2 NKJV)

The Story

1. Abraham had a son Ishmael, born by his female servant Hagar. This was before Isaac was born by Sarah, his wife.

2. Isaac was referred to as the child of promise.

3. Isaac grew up, and Abraham had a party for him.

4. Sarah observed that Ishmael was making fun of Isaac, and she did not like it.

5. As a result, Sarah told Abraham to send him and his mother away.

6. Abraham was not happy because of what Sarah said but God instructed him to do what his wife had said.

7. Abraham sent Ishmael and Hagar away but gave them food and water.

8. They were lost in the desert of Beersheba.

9. Later, when the water got finished. She put Ishmael under the shade of a tree because she thought he was going to die.

10. She cried, and the boy cried too, and God heard their cries.

11. An angel appeared to Hagar and told her that God had heard the cry of the boy.

12. God opened her eyes and she saw a well full of water.

13. She filled her container and gave it to the boy to drink.

14. The boy grew up and became successful.

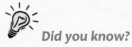

Did you know?

Abraham is the father of the Israel nation.

Meditation

1. Ishmael was the first son of Abraham, who was born by Hagar (Sarah's servant).

2. Eventually, when Isaac the child of promise was born and christened, Ishmael made fun of Isaac.

3. This was a bad thing to do, and he got in big trouble for it.

4. He and his mother were sent out of the house.

5. Ishmael became very thirsty in the desert because the water got finished and he was about to die.

6. Although he had done something bad, he and his mother cried

unto God and He answered their cries and provided water for them in the desert.

7. Have you ever landed in trouble for something you did wrong and you thought God would not care about you or love you anymore?

8. That is not true; it is a lie of the devil. God is merciful and is patiently waiting to hear your voice of repentance.

9. He wants you to pray for His mercy and ask Him for help.

10. He will forgive you your sins and open your eyes to opportunities you never thought were there just when you need them.

11. God always comes through in the nick of time.

12. He is never early or late.

13. He comes right on time.

Reflection:
In which situation do
I need God's timely help?

Prayer

Heavenly Father, I know I sometimes get into trouble for the wrong things I have done and keep doing. I ask that you forgive me all my sins and give me the grace not to go back to those sins again. Also, please help my friends and I in any difficult situations we find ourselves in Jesus' name. Amen

Printed in Great Britain
by Amazon